CH

SPIRIT-RAISING CHEERS AND CHANTS

BY MARCIA AMIDON LUSTED

CONTENT CONSULTANT

Pauline Zernott
Spirit Director and Coach
Louisiana State University

SportsZone
An Imprint of Abdo Publishing | abdopublishing.com

ABDOPUBLISHING.COM

Published by Abdo Publishing, a division of ABDO, PO Box 398166, Minneapolis, Minnesota 55439. Copyright © 2016 by Abdo Consulting Group, Inc. International copyrights reserved in all countries. No part of this book may be reproduced in any form without written permission from the publisher. SportsZone™ is a trademark and logo of Abdo Publishing.

Printed in the United States of America, North Mankato, Minnesota
082015
012016

THIS BOOK CONTAINS RECYCLED MATERIALS

Cover Photo: Icon Sportswire/AP Images
Interior Photos: Aspen Photo/Shutterstock Images, 4–5, 6, 8–9, 12, 20–21, 24–25; Amy Myers/Shutterstock Images, 7; Christopher Futcher/iStockphoto, 10–11; Gene J. Puskar/AP Images, 14–15; Icon Sportswire/AP Images, 17, 19 (top and bottom); Phelan M. Ebenhack/AP Images, 18, 22; Pavel L Photo and Video/Shutterstock Images, 26; Cal Sport Media/AP Images, 27; Richard Paul Kane/Shutterstock Images, 28–29

Editor: Mirella Miller
Series Designer: Maggie Villaume

Library of Congress Control Number: 2015945770

Cataloging-in-Publication Data

Lusted, Marcia Amidon.
 Spirit-raising cheers and chants / Marcia Amidon Lusted.
  p. cm. -- (Cheerleading)
ISBN 978-1-62403-986-7 (lib. bdg.)
Includes bibliographical references and index.
1. Cheerleading--Juvenile literature.   I. Title.
791.6/4--dc23
                                                          2015945770

CONTENTS

ONE
GO
TEAM!

Part of the fun of sporting events is the excitement. And for many sports, cheerleaders play a big part in helping fans get excited. Cheerleaders perform routines with jumps and stunts. They also have chants and cheers that they yell. Sometimes cheerleaders get the fans involved in their chants. Everyone gets the chance to cheer and support the team.

Chants are rhythmic yells that are easy to repeat. They are also easy to remember. Chants are usually short. They are also repeated many times. A chant might be about the sport. Or it might be about the school and its mascot. Some chants are special cheers about certain players.

When the fans have a lot of energy, it can help the team play better.

Yelling loudly gets both the cheerleaders and the fans excited!

Sometimes the crowd has its own part in a cheer.

Cheerleaders yell chants together at the same time. When a cheerleading team chants in unison, it makes the cheer louder and more energetic. It encourages the players and shows enthusiasm.

Chants fill in time between plays in a game, when fans are waiting for more action. Cheerleaders help keep the energy level high even when nothing is happening in the game. Chants are often performed before the game or at halftime. They also add to cheerleading routines. There are special chants to be yelled from the sidelines of a field. Others are done on the field during game breaks. Some chants are yelled as a call and response between cheerleaders and fans. Each group yells its own part.

YELL SQUADS

YELL SQUADS

Cheerleading started in the 1890s with yells. At the University of Minnesota, a student named Johnny Campbell wanted to support his sports teams. He led "yell squads" for his school. He directed other students to yell and chant together. These first yell squads were made up of all men.

Cheers are a little different from chants because they are longer and are usually only said once. They are also said in unison by the cheer team. Yells are the simplest of all. They might be as simple as yelling "Go team!" or "Make noise!" They do not need to be practiced. Cheers and chants must be learned, just as cheerleading actions have to be learned. It takes a little work to perform chants and cheers well. It is important that chants can be heard and understood. But it is fun to practice different cheerleading chants!

TWO

YELL
IT OUT

Cheers and chants are a big part of cheerleading. Cheerleaders need to be able to perform them well. But there is more to cheers and chants than opening your mouth and yelling. Similar to singers, cheerleaders need to make sure they cannot only make a lot of noise but that they protect their voices too.

Cheers and chants are easy to perform loudly when a cheerleader is standing still. Most of the time, chants go along with routines that include moving, jumping, and stunting. This can make it hard to remember the words to a chant and yell it clearly for fans to hear what is being said.

Yelling cheers may look easy, but it takes a lot of practice.

Successful cheers and chants should come from the diaphragm, not the throat. The diaphragm is a dome-shaped muscle that sits underneath the lungs. When we breathe in the diaphragm contracts to make room for our lungs. The diaphragm then brings the ribs back when we exhale. Using the diaphragm when yelling cheers means standing up straight and breathing deeply from the stomach instead of the chest. One way to practice good breathing is to lie on your stomach and yell out cheers. This will help you feel what it is like to breathe from your stomach rather than yell from your throat.

It is not hard to remember the words to chants and cheers. Unlike songs on the radio, there is not music to help you remember them. But since they sometimes rhyme, the rhythm can make them easy to remember. Practice the words to chants and cheers every time you practice the cheerleading moves that go with them. This will help the words become automatic. Soon you will not have to think about them.

With practice the chants will be another part of your cheerleading routine.

THREE

A CHANT
FOR EVERYONE

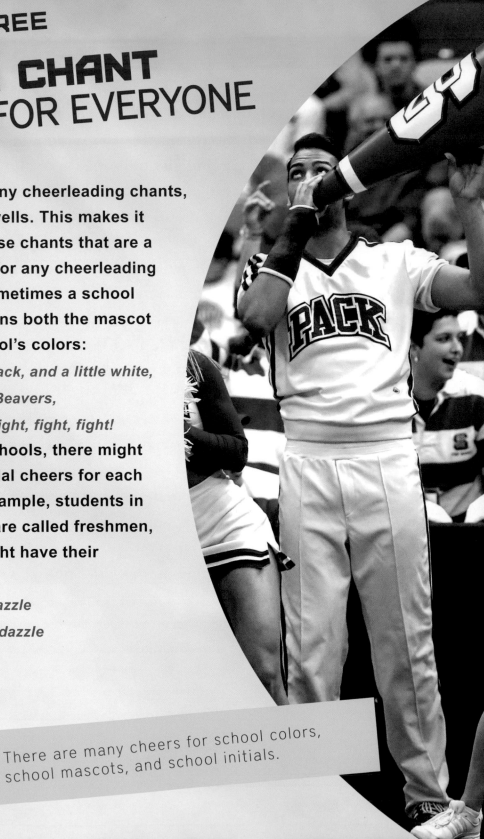

There are many cheerleading chants, cheers, and yells. This makes it easy to choose chants that are a good match for any cheerleading situation. Sometimes a school cheer mentions both the mascot and the school's colors:

Orange, black, and a little white,
We're the Beavers,
And we'll fight, fight, fight!

In high schools, there might also be special cheers for each class. For example, students in ninth grade are called freshmen, and they might have their own cheer:

Razzle, snazzle
Freshmen dazzle

There are many cheers for school colors, school mascots, and school initials.

Many cheers are done as a back-and-forth, which is also known as call and response. This means the leader calls out a line, and the rest of the cheerleading team calls out the next line in response:

Leader: *Everywhere we go*

Everyone: *Everywhere we go*

L: *People wanna know*

E: *People wanna know*

L: *Who we are*

E: *Who we are*

L: *And where we come from*

E: *And where we come from*

L: *So we tell them*

E: *So we tell them*

L: *We are the (insert team name)*

E: *The mighty mighty (team name)*

Sometimes cheerleaders hold signs with the words for the crowd to yell.

CALL AND RESPONSE

Sometimes a cheerleading team splits into two groups. Then they do call-and-response chants. The school mascot may join in. Your school may have a mascot costume that someone wears at every game or pep rally. Some common mascots include tigers, eagles, bears, or characters such as Spartan warriors, knights, or Vikings. The mascot is usually the school's symbol.

Call and response can be done with the fans, if they know the cheer.

Cheerleaders might mime actions to go along with a chant.

The mascot can also join in the fun and get the crowd excited.

FOUR

A CHANT FOR EVERY SPORT

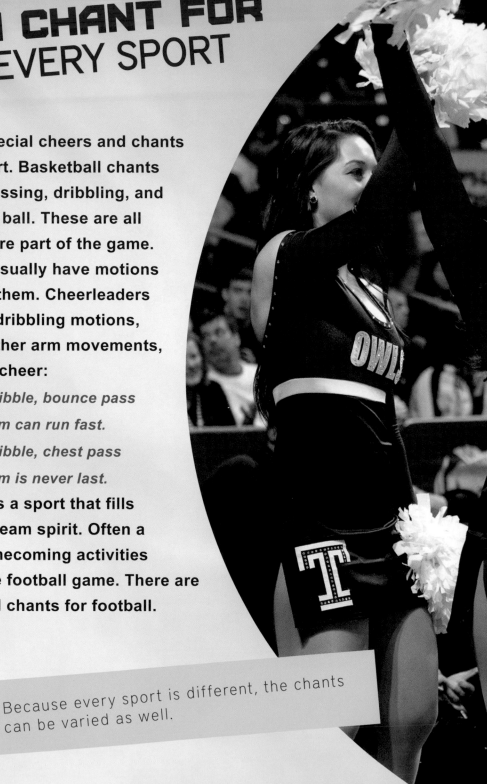

There are special cheers and chants for each sport. Basketball chants talk about passing, dribbling, and shooting the ball. These are all moves that are part of the game. The chants usually have motions that go with them. Cheerleaders might make dribbling motions, along with other arm movements, as they do a cheer:

Dribble, dribble, bounce pass
Eagles team can run fast.
Dribble, dribble, chest pass
Eagles team is never last.

Football is a sport that fills people with team spirit. Often a school's homecoming activities center on the football game. There are many special chants for football.

Because every sport is different, the chants can be varied as well.

Hockey cheerleaders go on the ice before the game and in between periods.

Hockey games can also have cheerleaders and special cheers and chants. They have cheers for moving the puck down the ice, shooting, and scoring:

Pass, skate, shoot to score.

Make a goal, we want more!

1–2–3–4

Shoot the puck.

Come on, let's score!

Fans in the stands,

Let me hear you clap your hands.

We're ready to win, we're ready to fight.

Now shoot that puck down the ice!

FIVE

THE OLD
AND THE NEW

The best way to cheer for a team at an event is to use a mix of old and new chants. Fans and team members can join in with the old chants. But new chants keep things fresh and keep the energy high. Fans are excited when they hear new chants and see different routines.

It is easy to find new chants. With an adult's help, find a cheerleading website that has a large collection of chants. Listening to the cheers and chants of visiting teams' cheerleaders is another way to find new material.

It can be fun to try out new cheers with an excited crowd.

Competition judges appreciate creativity and fresh material.

Cheerleading competitions are also a good source for chants. Many cheer teams use new chants during competitions, because it gives them an advantage over other teams. If your cheer team participates in a competition, writing new cheers and chants will give you the same edge.

It is not difficult to write new cheerleading cheers and chants. If you have team members who are good at writing poetry, they can help. Cheers can be written by one person or as a group. Start by making a list of things that represent your school. They might be your school colors, your mascot, your school and town names, and anything special your school is known for. This can help you come up with lines to use in your cheers.

Signs and chants might include a saying the school is known for.

Cheers and chants do not have to rhyme, but they can if you want them to. They can be short or long. They can be yelled by the cheer team or as a call and response with fans. Cheers and chants should have a rhythm, so they are easy to remember and fun to say. You might even start with a certain rhythm, maybe borrowed from one of your team's favorite cheers, and then make up new lines to fit. It is fun to brainstorm as a group. Call out lines to each other and see what sounds good.

Cheers and chants are one of the best ways for cheerleaders to add fun and excitement to a game. They involve the fans, and a game is more fun when everyone is energetic and excited!

CHEERING ON YOUR TEAM

Remember, when you are making up chants for your team, you can make up chants for individual players too. Knowing they have the support of the cheerleaders and the fans will help them do their best.

It is fun to get the crowd involved in cheering!

GLOSSARY

DRIBBLING
To bounce a basketball while moving forward during a game.

HALFTIME
A break in the middle of a game, when there is often a show or event.

MASCOT
An animal, person, or thing that is a symbol of a school or group.

RESPONSE
A spoken or chanted reply during a cheer chant.

ROUTINES
A series of movements that are repeated for a performance.

STUNT
Exciting and sometimes dangerous moves or jumps done during a cheer routine.

FOR MORE
INFORMATION

BOOKS

Farina, Christine, and Courtney A. Clark. *The Complete Guide to Cheerleading: All the Tips, Tricks, and Inspiration.* Minneapolis, MN: MVP, 2011.

Webb, Margaret. *Pump It Up Cheerleading.* New York: Crabtree, 2012.

Webber, Rebecca. *Varsity's Ultimate Guide to Cheerleading.* New York: Little, 2014.

WEBSITES

To learn more about Cheerleading, visit **booklinks.abdopublishing.com**. These links are routinely monitored and updated to provide the most current information available.

INDEX

ABOUT THE AUTHOR

Marcia Amidon Lusted has written more than 100 books and 500 magazine articles for young readers on many different subjects, from animals to countries to rock groups. She is also an editor and a musician. She lives in New England.